THIS WE BELIEVE:

The Christian Case for

Gay Civil Rights

PRAISE FOR

This We Believe: The Christian Case for Gay Civil Rights

"This book is a veritable *CliffsNotes* on what we now know about homosexuality and its relationship to Christian faith. In a few short pages, C.S. Pearce debunks long-held myths, clarifies Scripture and argues for a much needed rethinking of the Church's traditional stand. Just reading these words will reassure young gay and lesbian people that God loves them just as they are, while challenging those who are not so sure that perhaps they have put God's love in too small a box. I welcome this fine and well-written resource for the Church."

—**Rt. Rev. V. Gene Robinson, Bishop of New Hampshire**

"This book by C.S. Pearce is a wonderful resource. The author has done a thorough job of gathering together information that I have found sadly lacking in many areas of Christendom."

—**Peggy Campolo, Christian advocate for those children of God who happen not to be straight**

"Many will read this book who find themselves unable to judge gay and lesbian people and who want to understand why that's the right response. Some will be unsure what to say, and they will find in these pages immensely helpful guidance. Still others who pick up the book will believe that homosexuality is always and everywhere sinful. You who start with that belief and yet read these chapters with an open mind have my highest respect. I trust you will recognize here that same message of compassion that you see also in the life of Jesus."

–Dr. Philip Clayton, Provost of Claremont Lincoln University and Dean of Claremont School of Theology, Claremont, Calif.

"C.S. Pearce's book should be read by all who wish to navigate through the misinformation used to religiously justify the persecution, abuse, and oppression of our gay brothers and sisters in Christ. She gets to the heart of the debate in a crisp, profound, and accessible manner. Enlightening for those seeking answers on how to respond to the 'Gay Debate' from a Christ-centered position."

–Rev. Dr. Miguel A. De La Torre, author of
A Lily Among the Thorns: Imagining a New Christian Sexuality,
**professor of social ethics at Iliff School of Theology,
Denver, Colorado, and Southern Baptist minister**

"*This We Believe* is an excellent resource for those who are willing to investigate Christian perspectives on homosexuality. C.S. Pearce succinctly presents the latest biblical, legal, psychological, and ethical research to help Christians think through the issues of gay civil rights in a highly accessible first look into the field. If you care about people and their suffering, you should read this book."

—Rev. Dr. Monica A. Coleman, associate professor of constructive theology and African American religions at Claremont School of Theology, Claremont, Calif., and African Methodist Episcopal minister

"C.S. Pearce doesn't waste a word in reclaiming God's love for LGBT young people. May they read *This We Believe: The Christian Case for Gay Civil Rights* and realize God loves them just the way they are. Then, may they share this little book with their friends, parents, other relatives, pastors, and fellow congregants. If enough people are exposed to this Spirit-filled common sense, Christianity will become an ally rather than an antagonist in the LGBT rights movement."

—John Cepek, board member and former national president of PFLAG - Parents, Families, and Friends of Lesbians and Gays (www.pflag.org)

"*This We Believe: The Christian Case for Gay Civil Rights* is an important contribution to bridging the divide over homosexuality in the church with compassion, clarity and grace. In this thorough and accessible book, C.S. Pearce offers us both a faith-based response to the myths that marginalize LGBT young people and hope that the hurting can stop and the healing begin. It should be a staple on every pastor's bookshelf."

—Rev. Canon Susan Russell, priest, All Saints Church, Pasadena, Calif., and former president of Integrity, the LGBT advocacy organization of the Episcopal Church

"C.S. Pearce's *This We Believe: The Christian Case for Gay Civil Rights* offers an informative, challenging, and compelling perspective on changing cultural and biblical understandings of homosexuality today. Regardless of one's biblical perspective, it is well worth the read."

—Rev. Joe Roos, co-founder of *Sojourners* magazine and Mennonite pastor

.

THIS WE BELIEVE:

The Christian Case for

Gay Civil Rights

C. S. PEARCE

POMONA PRESS
Claremont, California

POMONA PRESS
Claremont, California

This We Believe: The Christian Case for Gay Civil Rights

Cover design: Nicole Rose Dion
Interior design: Linda McAdoo Ware

Printed in the United States of America

Library of Congress Cataloging-in-Publication Data is available.

Paperback ISBN: 978-0-9883681-0-1
Ebook ISBN: 978-0-9883681-1-8

To Paul McCullough

With fond memories of that long-ago,

extremely awkward lunch on

National Coming Out Day

.

Contents

FOUR

THE PRIVILEGE OF FAMILY: JENNIFER CHRISLER INVITES TONY PERKINS TO DINNER 40

Gay people long for the same rights as straight people to create loving families that are legally recognized everywhere, and accorded the same privileges. Instead, their families are penalized by our laws in many ways.

FIVE

WHAT THE BIBLE SAYS 47

Not too much about homosexuality, as it turns out.

And Jesus never even brings it up.

Contents

SIX

Is It Really a Choice?   64

*In a word: No. Bisexuals do have choices about which sex
they date, but not who they fall in love with. Scientific
studies have demonstrated that sexual orientation is not a
matter of choice for either gay or straight people, and
that attempting to change it is harmful on many levels.*

SEVEN

What About "Ex-Gays"?   72

*Why groups that claim to help people become "ex-gay"
hurt those they're trying to help.*

EIGHT

Conclusion: Start the Healing   79

Contents

APPENDICES

ACKNOWLEDGMENTS

PREFACE

I was raised in a conservative evangelical family, and I never thought much about homosexuality until after I left college. Based on what I'd been taught, I assumed that homosexuality was a choice that creepy perverts made, and I didn't know anyone who was gay—or so I thought. Many years later I discovered that two of the most engaging people in the high school group I'd hung out with were gay. Back then, however, LGBT (lesbian, gay, bisexual, and transgender) people mostly stayed in the closet for their own protection, even in Southern California.

In the late 1980s however, I suddenly became more conscious of gay issues when one of my favorite coworkers took me to lunch and "came out" to me—appropriately enough, on National Coming Out Day. The signs that Paul was gay would probably have been obvious to many people, but I didn't catch on until he told me, because he was a sweet, smart person with a wry sense of humor; certainly not a "creepy pervert."

When Paul first told me the news, I felt extremely uncomfortable. But gradually I realized that not only had it taken great courage for him to come out, but also that he was the same person that he had been before. I began to re-examine my preconceptions. I even did research on homosexuality, because by the early 1990s, my husband, who had already finished his residency in internal medicine, had decided on HIV as his sub-specialty. Back then, AIDS was considered a death sentence. Not much was known about it, and many physicians were reluctant to treat people with AIDS, fearing they could become infected through casual contact. So the need for HIV doctors was great.

Paul was the first of my "out" gay friends. Over the years, my husband and I came to know many wonderful LGBT people. Their empathy for others and the grace and humor with which they faced life were very attractive—a direct result of learning to cope with all the prejudice and stigmatization that many of them had had to deal with as they grew up.

The saying "Whatever doesn't kill you makes you stronger" applied big time to these friends. Quite a few of them, especially those from conservative Christian families, told me that because they were not capable of being straight, they had contemplated suicide at certain points in their lives. The AIDS epidemic only made the stigma worse.

Many gay people had chosen to move to California to be far from the communities where they were raised, to live lives that were true to who they were. One of my best friends, for example, was a gifted pianist and a civilian physician for the Navy, and I'm sure that made his North Carolinian parents proud. But he never came out to them, and he resourcefully deflected any attempts they made to set him up with nice women when he went back East for rare visits. They went to their graves believing (or perhaps pretending) that the man he had lived with for so many years was just his roommate.

Today, things are significantly better for the LGBT community in the United States than they were back in the 1980s and 1990s. But there are many sincere Christians who still believe that God requires them to deny the gay community the same civil rights that they themselves take for granted. It is for these people that I wrote this book.

There is infinitely more that holds us together than that separates us. By claiming that name, Christian, we aspire to be Christ-like, to live in goodness and mercy, with compassion and kindness toward all. We may disagree on issues including this one, but I know very well that we have a shared sense of basic values.

In the name of the God of Love, I hope and pray that you will read this with an open mind. Today, our gay fellow citizens' future continues to be debated in the churches, on current ballot initiatives, and in the courts. We have the opportunity to use our faith to demonstrate compassion and courage, empathy and justice. May the love of Christ prevail.

C.S. Pearce is a California-based writer and director of media relations for Claremont School of Theology. She has received many honors for her magazine stories, including the Outstanding Magazine Article Award from San Diego's Gay & Lesbian Alliance Against Defamation in 1993 and 1995.

.

ONE

WHY THIS BOOK MATTERS

> Whoever welcomes a little child like this in my name welcomes
> me. But if anyone causes one of these little ones who believe in me
> to sin, it would be better for him to have a large millstone hung
> around his neck and to be drowned in the depths of the sea.
>
> —Matthew 18:5-6

Nearly all Christians agree that young people are vulnerable
and need guidance and protection. But what happens when
that guidance destroys young people's sense of self-worth,
makes them vulnerable to abuse, and leads them to contemplate suicide for relief from despair?

It is this book's contention that traditional Christian beliefs
about homosexuality are hurting all of the church, especially
its most vulnerable members: young gay people who are convinced that their very essence is sinful. The consequences are
tragic on many levels.

Please consider its arguments carefully. Because if the traditional Christian position on homosexuality is not support-
able on biblical, intellectual, or compassionate grounds, and

you continue to hold to it, you share in the responsibility for the consequences.

The next chapter examines these consequences. Chapter 3 scrutinizes common myths about homosexuality. Chapter 4 focuses on specific examples of the harm that the Defense of Marriage Act is doing to the two million children of LGBT couples, as well as their parents and the rest of the LGBT community.

Chapter 5 examines all of the biblical passages that have been used to condemn homosexuality (the so-called "clobber verses") in the light of current scholarship and the ministry of Jesus in the Gospels. It also addresses the question: "If this 'new' interpretation of the Bible is true, how could Christians have had it wrong all these years?"

Chapter 6 discusses whether being gay is a choice. And Chapter 7 looks at self-help groups that claim to help people become "ex-gay."

Although I wrote this book primarily for traditional Christians,* I hope that it will also help LGBT people and their friends who are about to give up on the church to reconsider: Don't write off Christianity quite yet. Top Bible scholars, an ever-growing number of denominations, and an even larger number of individual churches are saying, "This we believe: God loves the LGBT community just as much as the straight community and wants LGBT people to have the same rights and opportunities that straight people do, both in the church and in the world." We who believe this may still hold the minority position within Christianity, but that is changing rapidly—for very good reasons—and this book explains why.

* In this book, the phrase "traditional Christians" refers to the evangelicals, Catholics, Pentecostals, mainline Protestants, and other Christians who still believe homosexual behavior is a sin.

TWO

STOP THE HURT!

My God, my God, why have you forsaken me?
—Psalm 22:1, Mark 15:34

No one should be separated from the love of God. That is the wonderful message of the entire New Testament. By requiring that LGBT people change their very essence to be connected to that love, however, we're putting huge barriers between them and God. The traditional Christian position on homosexuality is a denial of the realities of God's creation that has negative and often tragic consequences:

SUICIDES

In her book *Prayers for Bobby*,[1] Mary Griffith recounts the heartbreaking story of her late son. She is painfully honest about her well-meaning but deadly complicity in his death at the age of 20. For years Bobby Griffith had sought healing from his homosexuality with heartfelt prayers, special therapy, and the encouragement and prodding of his mother. He finally committed suicide to escape his feelings of wretched sinfulness, because he believed God wouldn't or couldn't "heal" him. After his death, Griffith began to question her beliefs. "Looking back," she writes, "I realize how depraved it was to instill false guilt in an innocent child, causing a distorted image of life, God, and self, leaving little if any feeling of personal worth."

Unfortunately, Bobby's fate is not unique. LGBT teens are three to seven times more likely to commit suicide than straight teens, according to *Pediatrics* and the U.S. Surgeon General, [2] and it's much more likely to happen when they are bullied.

BULLYING

"Growing Up LGBT in America," a groundbreaking 2012 survey by the Human Rights Campaign of more than 10,000 LGBT teens, shows that non-heterosexual adolescents are significantly more likely to be verbally harassed and physically assaulted than their heterosexual peers. Homophobic bullying also affects kids who are not actually gay: Boys who aren't skilled in sports or who have effeminate traits are also called names like "homo" or "faggot" and are targets for physical harm. Girls who assert themselves, who don't care for especially feminine clothes, or who may not want to date or have sex with a star male athlete who is pressuring them are called "dykes" and "lesbos."

Older and more secure LGBT people have taken the sting out of such epithets by appropriating them. In more progressive areas, terms like queen (for a male), dyke, or queer may be used as a badge of honor and/or affection. For young people in less progressive areas, however, such terms are a mark of stigma and shame.

When gay youth are harassed at school and then attend a church that tells them that their very essence is evil—and have parents who believe the same—they have nowhere to turn. Here in California, a number of school boards have tried to give these children hope and protection by making discrimination based on sexual orientation illegal. Often, however, local Christians fight these measures. I once heard a father say, "Schools should not teach that homosexuality is normal, healthy, natural, moral, or acceptable. It is none of these things. But homosexuals should not be mistreated in any way. School bullies need to be held accountable."

He didn't see the extraordinary contradiction in his position: Children are not subtle; they see things in black and white. Tell them that homosexuality is evil, and if they think a classmate is gay, they will feel justified and even virtuous when they harass that person. And tell children who are attracted to the same sex that homosexuality is immoral and unnatural, and they will assume that they deserve the taunts and abuse that come their way—and will struggle with feelings of worthlessness and despair.

LOSS OF CHRISTIAN FAITH AND LOSS OF POTENTIAL

Many Christians now accept what the research of psychiatry and social science has proven: "Healing" people from their homosexuality simply doesn't work. Christian leaders who accept that fact, but still hold traditional views, will therefore advocate celibacy for gay people who want to follow God. So in order to remain Christian, their gay followers renounce the hope of ever having a partner in life.

Some repudiate their Christianity because it asks something impossible of them, and go on to live healthy lives in spite of the disapproval of their parents and former church. Often, however, they will miss their faith and their relationship with God, and eventually discover a more accepting fold. Many, however, never find a way back to Christianity.

Others, like Bobby Griffith, begin a long struggle against their sexuality: they pray fervently, go through therapy, sometimes marry a person of the opposite sex, join ex-gay groups, and feel miserable every time they have a lapse. Because they've had to grapple with self-loathing, they often don't achieve what they might have in life if they had simply been accepted for who they were. They, like others who battle depression and feelings of helplessness about situations they can't change, are more vulnerable to the temptation of "self-medicating" with alcohol or drugs.[3]

Certain "ex-gay" programs have claimed that LGBT people are more susceptible to substance abuse and suicidal behavior because they are gay. But clinical psychologist Mark Hatzenbuehler, writing in *Pediatrics*, the journal of the American Academy of Pediatrics, offers compelling evidence that such harmful behaviors are directly related to local cultural stigma, and nothing inherent in LGBT individuals. In his study, Hatzenbuehler indexed communities by the proportions of same-sex couples, schools with gay-straight alliances, and other indicators of support. He found that the more conservative communities, where there were fewer of these institutions, had an elevated risk of suicidal behavior among all young people, especially LGBT youth.

According to Hatzenbuehler, LGBT youth were five times more likely to attempt suicide than straight youth on average, but they were 20 percent more likely to do so in unsupportive environments compared to supportive environments. [4]

Older data also support these contentions. In June 2004, the U.S. Center for Disease Control and Prevention announced that teen suicides in the nation were down by 25 percent over the previous decade. The Center attributed a major part of the reduction to the decrease in our society's stigma against homosexuality, including the fact that gay teens could now see gay people in the media and know that they were not alone. [2]

DOOMED MARRIAGES AND RISK OF SEXUALLY TRANSMITTED DISEASES

Too often, gay men and women who are Christian will marry someone of the opposite sex whom they love as a good friend, hoping that marriage will help them "go straight" and better fit in with society. Some churches and ex-gay groups actually encourage this. But when these marriages end in divorce, the same groups blame the "gay agenda" for the problem instead of themselves. If gay people could marry the people they actually love, such doomed mismatches wouldn't happen as often.

Ideally a gay person who plans to marry someone of the opposite sex will be open with that person, acknowledging their struggle, so their partner will enter the marriage informed and prepared. But many are in such denial that they don't warn the spouse. That makes the inevitable problems of such a union even worse. Straight spouses may feel unattractive, inferior, or guilty for not being able to physically attract their partner. Meanwhile, the sexually frustrated gay spouse may engage in secret liaisons that put both partners at risk for sexually transmitted diseases. African-Americans call this behavior the down low, and often the men who do it don't think of themselves as gay.[5] It is one of several reasons for the steep increase in HIV infections in communities of color, where the stigma against homosexuality as well as AIDS is often strong.[5]

The straight partner deserves a husband or wife who is straight, and the gay partner deserves a gay spouse. It's cruel to expect a gay person to either marry a member of the opposite sex or not marry at all; it's equally cruel to expect a heterosexual to be the other half of an alliance that denies both partners emotional and physical fulfillment.

DENIED THE RIGHT TO MARRY, DISCOURAGED FROM MONOGAMY

Therefore it is also cruel to put so many roadblocks in the way of gay people who fall in love and want to establish a lifelong partnership, something that most people yearn for. It's not easy to sustain a good marriage over many years. With all the barriers in their way, it's amazing that so many gay couples manage to create and keep loving unions, true marriages in all but name, that are excellent examples for any committed couple, straight or gay.

If a gay Christian who is attempting to become straight, or a gay Christian still in the closet is caught in a "homosexual lapse" and confesses, he or she is forgiven and encouraged to keep to the straight path. These people often suffer many such lapses over the course of their lives, but if they are skilled at hiding them, they are honored as good Christians. Meanwhile, gay couples who commit to a permanent, monogamous love relationship are told they are defying God and can no longer be called Christians. Thus the traditional Christian position actually discourages monogamy.

Gay and lesbian couples who wish to legally marry must hire a lawyer and pay substantial fees to get the legal protections that straight couples get automatically, such as inheritance and hospital visitation rights. Often gay people cannot get spousal insurance benefits from their partner's work-insurance policies, something else that most married couples take for granted.

Yet many traditional Christians and Mormons continue to push for amendments to ban same-sex marriage in their state and at the national level. At this writing, 30 states have passed constitutional amendments defining marriage as being between one man and one woman. The most recent was North Carolina, whose citizens voted for a constitutional amendment to ban same-sex marriage and civil unions, although it already had a law against same-sex marriages.

North Carolina even denies the non-biological parent the right to adopt their children as the second parent. So, for example, when a gay couple's child is hospitalized, and the child's non-biological parent wants to visit to give comfort and love, the parents must spend thousands of dollars to get legal papers to permit hospital visits, as well as pay for legal documents to give that parent permission to pick up the couple's children from school or take them to doctor's appointments. If the parents can't afford those legal costs, the children are left without access to either parent when their biological parent is incapacitated or dies. This is extremely hurtful to the children, who love and depend on their parents as much as children of straight couples love and depend on theirs.

As someone who was all too familiar with discrimination, the late Coretta Scott King, widow of Martin Luther King Jr., was appalled by the initiatives against marriage and family equality. Up until her death in 2006, she fought tirelessly for equal rights for gay people. "Like Martin, I don't believe you can stand for freedom for one group of people and deny it to others," she said at a June 23, 1994 Washington, D.C., press conference for the Employment Non-Discrimination Act passed that year.

"A constitutional amendment banning same-sex marriages is a form of gay bashing, and it would do nothing at all to protect traditional marriages," she told an audience at Richard Stockton College, in Pomona, New Jersey, on March 23, 2004.

On May 19, 2012, the NAACP (National Association for the Advancement of Colored People) Board of Directors also endorsed marriage equality, stating that it was a matter of ensuring the "political, educational, social, and economic equality of all people."

LIVING A LIE: PART 1

One of the most ironic things about being gay in much of the Christian church is that, whether you are a pastor or a layperson, if you hide your homosexuality, you can have a very effective ministry. If you come out, however, you are treated like a pariah, even though you are exactly the same person as you were before, but telling the truth instead of living a lie.

Jay Michaelson asks in his excellent book *God vs. Gay?*, "Imagine lying to everyone you know, all the time. Imagine feeling that your soul is distorted, evil, and broken. And imagine believing that, because of something you cannot change, God hates you. What would you do?"

Michaelson is Jewish, but the demons of the closet are the same no matter which religion you come from. For a long time he hid his sexuality and even considered ending his life. When he finally came out and joined an accepting religious community, the joy and relief he experienced were life changing, and he was able to write his powerful argument for equality, not despite religion, but because of it.

One of the most loving, effective, and Christ-like leaders I've met is the Episcopal bishop of New Hampshire, Gene Robinson. In November 2003, he was consecrated as a bishop in front of 3,500 people. There was such a phenomenal outpouring of love that witnesses who were present said it could literally be felt. Because of numerous death threats, however, Robinson wore a bulletproof vest under his robes and was flanked by bodyguards. The death threats were because Robinson had been open about his long-term partner, Mark Andrew.

Many Episcopal bishops were initially on the fence about voting to confirm Robinson's election. Some were concerned about the morality of electing an openly gay bishop; others were worried it might split the church. Several bishops pointed out, however, that had Robinson kept his homosexuality a secret, he would have been elected as a bishop years earlier because he was such a beloved and effective leader. But he had not been willing to lie about who he was in order to fulfill his calling. So they argued Robinson should be honored for his bravery in telling the truth, as well as for the extensive fruit of his ministry that had amply proven him called to God's work. To its credit, the Episcopal Church decided it was time to stop cutting off the body of Christ from the gifts of Christians who are gay and lesbian.

However, more than 20 churches upset about Gene Robinson's election removed themselves from the authority of the Episcopal Church's presiding bishop and joined the Church of Nigeria instead. In order to give them this option,

Nigeria's presiding archbishop, Peter Akinola, who views homosexuality as an abomination akin to bestiality and pedophilia, flew to the United States in 2007 to install one of the priests of the seceding congregations as a bishop of the Nigerian Church in America. This visit came on the heels of Akinola's 2006 "Message to the Nation" of Nigeria in support of a bill that made homosexual sex and any public expression of homosexual identity a crime punishable by five years in prison.

None of the 20 seceding churches reported to Bishop Robinson or was required to have him lead their services. But their leaders believed that leaving the American fold for that of Archbishop Akinola's was a choice that Christ would approve.

LIVING A LIE: PART 2

If you follow the news, you can't help but notice the never-ending parade of high-profile anti-gay crusaders caught in compromising same-sex positions: Evangelical minister Ted Haggard's alleged three-year relationship with a male prostitute, Young Republican leader Glenn Murphy Jr. allegedly performing oral sex on a sleeping man, Idaho Senator Larry Craig allegedly soliciting sex in an airport bathroom, and the list goes on.

We now know the reason for their bizarre behavior. The

April 6, 2012 issue of *Science News* featured a series of studies showing that homophobia—which was defined as an intense and visceral fear of homosexuals—is more pronounced in people with an unacknowledged attraction to the same sex, who grew up with authority figures who condemned such desires.

"In many cases these are people who are at war with themselves, and they are turning this internal conflict outward," said Richard Ryan, professor of psychology at the University of Rochester, who was quoted in the story.

Such people risk losing the love and approval of their authority figures if they admit to their orientation, so they repress that part of themselves to the point of becoming strongly homophobic. Some indulge in bullying and hate crimes against those who are LGBT. Others become church leaders or legislators who institute anti-gay legislation and policies that worsen the oppression of their own unacknowledged community.

If society ceased stigmatizing homosexuality, all LGBT people, including those from conservative backgrounds, would be able to accept their essential nature, instead of fearing and repressing it. Then these kinds of oppressive behaviors would eventually disappear.

THREE

EXPOSING THE MYTHS

Then you will know the truth, and the truth will set you free.
— John 8:32

A lesbian friend once told me that "some of the most repulsive and blatant lies" she had heard about homosexuality were told in the Bible study classes she had attended. Too often, and usually unknowingly, Christians spread myths about gay people that cause others to fear and stigmatize them. Yet most of these hurtful and slanderous beliefs are easy to disprove. They continue to be propagated only because those who adopt them do so uncritically, without trying to find out whether they are actually true.

MYTH 1: "HOMOSEXUALS ARE PEDOPHILES"

It is true that some pedophiles are men who sexually abuse

boys. The most notorious cases in this country involved a number of priests in the Catholic Church, who were not prosecuted until recently. Because of them, some people equate homosexuality with pedophilia. In fact, there are many more male pedophiles who abuse girls, yet no one claims that all heterosexual males are pedophiles. It is illogical and extraordinarily harmful to slander gay men by saying homosexuals are pedophiles.[6]

Ironically, fear of homosexuality can also cause some gay men to sexually assault other gay men, as "Living a Lie: Part 2" explains. However, the vast majority of men who sexually assault male adults and children are heterosexual. In *Men Who Rape: The Psychology of the Offender* (New York: Plenum Press, 1980) Nicholas Groth and Jean Birnbaum state that in all of the rape cases they studied, for the perpetrators, "the sexual assault was an act of retaliation, an expression of power, and an assertion of their strength and manhood," and had nothing to do with their sexual orientation.

Some anti-gay groups cite the claims of Paul Cameron and his Family Research Institute that gay men are more likely to be child molesters than straight men. However, Cameron's claims have been widely discredited. He has been censured by numerous organizations for his false and distorted methodologies: He was expelled from the American Psychological Association in 1983, the Nebraska Psychological Association repudiated his work in 1984, the American Sociological Association condemned his consistent misrepresentation of sociological research in 1986, and the Canadian Psychological Association formally disassociated itself from him based on his "consistently misinterpreted and misrepresented research" in August 1996. Finally, on April 28, 2005, the *Wall Street Journal* ran an article exposing some of the leaps of logic and non-scientific techniques Cameron uses to arrive at his statistically invalid conclusions about gay people.[6]

Myth 2: "Homosexuality Is Caused by Poor Family Dynamics, Feelings of Being an Outsider and Sexual Abuse or Incest"

Unfortunately, many children grow up with poor family dynamics and feelings of not belonging. However, there is no credible evidence that such children are more likely to be gay. "Not natural, due to poor family dynamics," is an old-fashioned argument that was discredited by social scientists and

psychiatrists in the 1960s and early 1970s. The theory origi-
nated with Sigmund Freud and others who hypothesized,
based on some of the families they had observed in their
practice, that distant fathers and overprotective mothers led
to homosexual sons. Later, when that theory didn't pan out
statistically, researchers proposed that Freud was seeing the
effect of homosexuality rather than its cause, since in his era,
a father might well grow distant toward a son he saw as feminine, which might cause the boy's mother to become more
protective.

Such claims confuse cause with effect—in particular the
claim that feelings of being an outsider can cause homosexuality. Feeling like an outsider is a result of being gay, not a
cause of it. If you are gay, unless you are blessed enough to
grow up in a family and a place where being gay is acceptable,
you are guaranteed to feel like an outsider, given the stigma
that still exists in society in general, and the church specifically.

Amazingly, several prominent evangelical groups are still
repeating the widely discredited claim that strong mothers
and weak or absent fathers produce gay sons. Not only does
this place an unfair burden of guilt on parents who erro-
neously believe their child's homosexuality is a problem, it is

extremely illogical. If it were true, all boys raised by single mothers or who had absent fathers would be gay, including many boys raised in inner cities.

Incest and sexual abuse can cause severe problems for the victim—fear of or distaste for intimacy and sexual dysfunction, as well as depression and other complications. To say it causes homosexuality, however, is inaccurate. If every girl who was abused or raped became gay, almost a third of the women in the world would be lesbian.[7]

Girls who are abused by men may have difficulty feeling attracted to men later in life. If they happen to be bisexual or gay, living as lesbians will work for them, even if they don't work through the emotions and feelings of violation caused by the abuse. Heterosexual women, however, whose natures do not present that option, will often need therapy in order to overcome an aversion to sexual contact with men.

Similarly, gay boys who are molested by men may hate their feelings of attraction to men and may believe, in error, that the molestation caused their homosexuality. But such thinking and teaching complicates their recovery from the abuse. If they are truly gay, they will often need therapy to feel comfortable with their attraction to men.

MYTH 3: "THE HOMOSEXUAL LIFESTYLE"

According to the more lurid anti-gay propaganda that I've seen over the years, the "homosexual lifestyle" consists of partying at sadomasochistic-themed bars, drinking, taking drugs, and having unprotected sex with multiple partners. Tracts and videos depicting this behavior can be very effective for generating fear and outrage against LGBT people—and for raising large sums of money for the organizations that distribute them, usually organizations that identify as Christian.

In fact, there *are* gay people who have this lifestyle. There are also straight people whose heterosexual lifestyles are equally debauched. In the case of both heterosexuals and homosexuals, such heedless hedonism is a minority behavior. No one runs videos of drunken straight men at Las Vegas strip clubs leering at their topless lap-dancers, for example, and claims that they illustrate the "heterosexual lifestyle." So how do organizations get so many Christians to believe that the over-the-top behaviors they describe are the definitive homosexual lifestyle?

When a young friend of mine came out to her grandparents, she had been living with the woman she loved for four years, and they had decided to have a wedding to pledge faithfulness " 'til death do us part." Because of her grandparents' background, it was a big step for her to risk sharing the love of her life with them. When she did, her grandparents told her they loved her but did not approve of "the gay lifestyle." She replied that she wasn't sure what they meant by the gay lifestyle, but that she'd had a lot of pain in her life and that it was wonderful to finally have someone who loved and understood her as she was.

She didn't mention the obvious fact that most of her pain had been caused by the religious beliefs of her parents and grandparents. The woman she married is a wonderful person and extremely accomplished. If she were male, my friend's parents would be thrilled that their daughter had found her. Yet her father still calls their relationship "an abomination" (Lev. 18:22), although he eats shellfish (Lev. 11:10,11) and does several other things that the book of Leviticus cites as abominations. He also has a tattoo, which Lev. 19:28 forbids. Yet he doesn't see the hypocrisy in using selective Bible literalism to condemn his daughter and her wife while ignoring verses in the same book that condemn his own behavior. The section in Chapter 3 on the Old Testament goes into more detail about these ancient laws, which condemn many actions we consider harmless, yet don't condemn immoral activities like slavery.

MYTH 4: "OPENLY GAY TROOPS ARE BAD FOR MILITARY MORALE"

As of this book's publication, gay and lesbian troops serve openly in the armed forces of 44 nations, including Israel, Britain, Australia and Canada. In spite of predictions to the contrary, none of these countries report morale or recruitment problems because of this policy.

With the repeal of "Don't Ask, Don't Tell" (DADT) in September 2011, the United States became one of the most recent nations to allow gay people to serve openly.

"Today, with implementation of the new law fully in place, we are a stronger joint force, a more tolerant joint force, a force of more character and more honor, more in keeping with our own values," said Admiral Michael Mullen, who was then chairman of the Joint Chiefs of Staff, as he announced the repeal. "It was fundamentally against everything we stand for as an institution to force people to lie about who they are just to wear a uniform," Mullen continued. "We are better than that."

A number of politicians and some military leaders spoke publicly against the repeal, saying it would undermine unit cohesion, particularly among troops serving in combat. That has not happened.

At this writing, Defense Secretary Leon Panetta and other military leaders have reported that none of the military assessment reports so far show negative effects on military order or discipline from the repeal. In fact, according to a Nov. 28, 2011 *Marine Corps Time*s article, Marine Corps Commandant General Jim Amos, who spoke out against the repeal in December 2010, has admitted that his concerns were unfounded, and the repeal had turned out to be a "non-event."

Not surprisingly, morale is tremendously high among gay troops. They no longer have to live with the constant fear of being outed and then dismissed from serving their country. Lieutenant Gary Ross, a 2002 graduate of the Naval Academy, is one of the many who are rejoicing. He married his partner, civilian Dan Swezy, in Vermont just after midnight when DADT ended.

Now, he says, he doesn't have to pretend he's something he's not any more. "Being in the military is extremely invasive," he said in an Associated Press article. "It becomes a web of excuses you make when you try to be as honest as possible but can't be honest. ... If you're standing watch at midnight on a surface ship, there's not much to talk about. It becomes very difficult to trust someone you can't be honest with."

In public celebrations, on Facebook pages, in blogs, op-eds, and e-mails, the gay troops' outpouring of gratitude and relief at being able to be themselves and acknowledge their same-sex partners has been truly inspiring.

It has also saved the country millions of dollars. In a *New York Times* opinion piece published on September 13, 2010, a year before the DADT repeal, former United States Army Captain Jonathan Hopkins wrote, "Since the 1993 law known as 'don't ask, don't tell' was enacted by Congress, more than 14,000 gay service members have been discharged, at a cost to taxpayers of $464 million over the last decade. I am one of them. I was discharged just one month ago."

Hopkins graduated fourth in his class at West Point. He was deployed three times to lead platoons in Iraq and Afghanistan, earning three Bronze Star Medals, including one for valor. Then in 2009, at the same time his commanding officer told him he was being nominated to be a major a year earlier than usual because of his exemplary service, the officer also told him he was required to investigate a charge that Hopkins was gay. Hopkins decided not to fight it and admitted that he was indeed gay. It took 14 months for the army to process him out.

"Four months after being found out, and 10 months prior

to leaving the Army," Hopkins wrote, "I found myself with a boyfriend for the first time in my life, because I was no longer scared to have such a relationship. He and I attended social events and dinners with my peers. I talked about him at work. My life became one of full disclosure.

"Amid all of that, the unit continued to function and I continued to be respected for the work I did. Many, from both companies I commanded, approached me to say that they didn't care if I was gay—they thought I was one of the best commanders they'd ever had. And unbeknownst to me, many had guessed I was probably gay all along. Most didn't care about my sexuality. I was accepted by most of them, as was my boyfriend, and I had never been happier in the military. Nothing collapsed, no one stopped talking to me, the Earth spun on its axis, and the unit prepared to fight another day."

Fortunately, DADT's demise means the military is no longer losing exemplary soldiers like Hopkins. There are still hurdles to be overcome before true equality is achieved, however. At this writing, a Navy proposal to train chaplains to conduct same-sex civil unions in states where they are legal was under review by the Pentagon after some members of Congress objected to it. Same-sex military spouses still do not receive access to their partner's health insurance or to support groups when their loved one is deployed.

MYTH 5: "ALLOWING SAME-SEX MARRIAGE UNDERMINES THE INSTITUTION"

The arguments detailing why same-sex marriage would undermine the institution of marriage are addressed at the end of this section. None of them even remotely justifies the claim.

I've been married for 38 years, and my husband and I know a number of gay couples who have been together as long or even longer than we have. They have always supported our marriage, as we have theirs. There are good marriages and deficient marriages, and we learn from the examples of one and the mistakes of the other—it doesn't matter if the partners are of the same or opposite gender.

One of the most committed marriages I know of is an elementary school teacher and a professor who have been together more than 38 years. For the first 20 years of their marriage, they were equals. They respected each other, were witty and loving, and were magnets for friends and people who wanted someone to confide in. The teacher had been

HIV-positive since his younger days but was one of the fortunate few who had not fallen ill during that time.

Years later, when he developed AIDS, he almost died of toxoplasmosis, but survived with brain damage. Now he is a good-looking middle-aged man, but he acts like a child: sometimes wetting his pants, asking lots of questions, and so on. His partner, the professor, was devastated, of course. But he has stuck by his spouse all these years, and is as loving as ever. His devotion to this child in a man's body is awe-inspiring—a demonstration of love in its highest form.

Would I be able to cope as well, living with my husband if he were in the same situation? I honestly don't know and hope I never have to find out. Meanwhile, I have yet to find a sound reason behind the claim that same-sex marriage undermines the institution of marriage or destroys families.

In 2004, Massachusetts became the first of our states to legalize same-sex marriage, and today it has one of the lowest divorce rates in the nation. As of this writing, five additional states and Washington, D.C., have also legalized same-sex marriages, and none has seen an uptick in heterosexual divorces.

True love seems to be truly gender blind, even in the poetry that couples choose to have quoted during their weddings.

Straight couples who pick a W. H. Auden love sonnet for their ceremony, for example, might not realize that Auden was writing about his male partner, because his poetry illuminates such universal feelings.

The following are the three most common reasons given to support the idea that same-sex marriage would undermine the institution of marriage, and none explains why or how the undermining would take place.

"God created Adam and Eve, not Adam and Steve." According to Genesis, God's first reason for creating Eve was that Adam needed companionship. His second reason was so that humanity could "multiply and fill the earth." If reproduction were actually meant as a command for all people, then anyone who remained single and did not multiply—including Jesus and Paul—would be sinning. Furthermore, humans have filled the earth more than adequately, and today many people no longer believe that bearing children is the main purpose of marriage. The need for companionship and intimacy is still extremely strong for most people, however, and to deny it to gay people is simply cruel.

"Marriage is between a man and a woman." This has been a long-time tradition, but sometimes there are compelling reasons to move beyond traditions. For many centuries in many cultures, including that of the Old Testament, monogamous marriages based on love were not the norm. Marriages were political, dynastic, and financial transactions, and women were considered property. The father or parents arranged the marriages, and polygamy was common. For various reasons, each of these long-time marriage traditions changed. And justice and compassion demand that it's time to change the current "between a man and a woman only" tradition too.

"If gay people can marry, they'll legally be allowed to have children." This is true, but many gay people already have children—and will continue to. There are about one million same-sex couples parenting two million children in America today, according to the 2010 Census. Furthermore, psychologists and sociologists point out that research demonstrates that, if possible, it's better for a child to have two committed parents than one. Since marriage has been proven to increase commitment, it would make sense to allow these couples to marry for the sake of their children, as well as for all other reasons of basic justice and fairness.

Clearly, allowing gay parents to marry would be beneficial for their children, but opponents of gay marriage often cite studies that supposedly show that children do better when they are raised by a "mother and a father." The studies to which they are referring, however, are studies of heterosexual parents. When the studies include same-sex parents in the mix, they show that children do better when they are raised by two parents instead of one, regardless of the sex of the parents. Because claims that same-sex couples make inferior parents are so common, they are covered as a separate myth below.

Myth 6: "Same-Sex Couples Don't Make Good Parents"

During the 2012 election primaries, Republican presidential candidate Rick Santorum emotionally claimed that it was better for a child to have a father in prison than to have same-sex parents. He justified this statement by citing an antipoverty expert who found, according to Santorum, "that even fathers in jail who had abandoned their kids were still better than no father at all to have in their children's lives."

Allowing same-sex parents to marry and raise children is, Santorum continued, "robbing children of something they need, they deserve, they have a right to."

No one seems to know exactly which study Santorum was

talking about. Is it one of the anti-gay pseudoscience studies?[6] If not, if it is a valid, peer-reviewed study, then he must be misinterpreting the results. Several legitimate peer-reviewed studies have shown that two parents are better than one, even when one parent is in prison. These studies examined heterosexual couples versus a single mother with no father in the picture; hence the statement about fathers.

The claim that same-sex parenting hurts children has been proven absolutely false by every long-term social science study comparing the children of same-sex parents with the children of mixed-sex parents. In fact, if the two parents are women, their children are likely to have an even better chance of success and happiness in life than their peers with a mother and a father, according to the June 2010 issue of the journal *Pediatrics*. It published a ground-breaking study by Nanette Gartrell, MD, titled "USA National Longitudinal Lesbian Family Study: Psychological Adjustment of the 17-Year-Old Adolescents." It was the longest-running and largest investigation of lesbian mothers and their children in America and received international media attention.

The study's results stand diametrically opposite to Santorum's claim: The 17-year-old sons and daughters of lesbian couples rated significantly higher in social, academic, and total competence than their age-matched counterparts, and showed significantly lower levels of social problems, rule-breaking, aggressiveness, and other problem behavior.

There is no longer any question that same-sex parents are no better or no worse for children than their heterosexual counterparts. So why do groups like Focus on the Family and the Family Research Council, as well as politicians like Santorum, continue to insist the opposite is true?

In a Viewpoint column against gay parenting published in the December 18, 2006, issue of *Time* magazine titled "Two Mommies Is One Too Many," Focus on the Family leader James Dobson wrote, "The majority of more than 30 years of social-science evidence indicates that children do best on every measure of well-being when raised by their married mother and father." He went on to cite the work of Kyle Pruett, MD, of Yale Medical School and educational psychologist Carol Gilligan, PhD, to substantiate his point. What he did not add—and unfortunately, *Time* did not point out—is that he was completely misrepresenting the studies he referenced when he applied them to gay parents. In fact, all of the researchers mentioned by Dobson have refuted his misrepresentations of their research.[8]

"All of the studies [Dobson cited] compared heterosexual

parents in one form or another," said New York University professor of sociology Judith Stacey, Ph.D., who coauthored some of these studies. She made her statements on a YouTube interview, which she scheduled in hopes that it would undo some of the damage done by Dobson. She explained that the research examined heterosexual parents who were divorced, married, or had children outside of marriage and that was the context of the conclusion that "Children do best when raised with a committed mother and a father." She went on to explain that when such studies include gay parents in the mix, researchers find that a child is better off with two committed parents, no matter what the parents' sex.

In fact, Stacey said, children of gay parents do slightly better overall than those of heterosexual parents, a finding she attributed to the fact that gay parents are more likely to make their decision to bear and/or raise children more consciously.[8] Stacey was especially disturbed that Focus on the Family has cited distorted versions of her heterosexual studies as evidence in court cases to prevent gay couples from having parental rights, and, as she explained in the YouTube interview, she has had to spend quite a bit of time responding with affidavits to set the record straight.[8]

"When people start spinning science you have to respond," said Yale's Pruett. "Journalism used to handle this, but not anymore. So it's bounced back to become increasingly the responsibility of the people doing the research."[8]

In 2005, the American Psychological Association concluded that "not a single study has found children of lesbian or gay parents to be disadvantaged in any significant respect relative to children of heterosexual parents," and many later studies confirmed this finding.[9,10] Yet politicians such as Santorum and groups such as Focus on the Family continue to misrepresent these studies in order to cast aspersions on gay parents. By doing so, they are hurting both these parents and their children.

TAKING IT TO THE COURTS

Proposition 8 is a California state constitutional amendment that eliminated the previously established right of same-sex couples to marry. During the 2008 campaign, Prop 8 supporters ran a flood of ads with negative claims about same-sex marriage. Prop 8 opponents, who were initially ahead in the polls, were caught unaware by the number and intensity of these ads and, frankly, didn't do a good job of refuting them. So the measure passed with 52 percent of the vote.

When the opponents regrouped and brought Prop 8 to trial for being unconstitutional, however, the defense couldn't find any legitimate scientists who would verify under oath the supporters' campaign claims about the alleged harm caused by same-sex marriage. Even the scientific witness for the defense reluctantly admitted that same-sex marriage would likely improve the well being of families of same sex couples and their children. According to trial transcripts, this witness had actually previously published work in which he had said, "We would be more American on the day that we permitted same-sex marriage than we had been the day before."

Because the defenders of Prop 8 defense could not come up with any credible evidence or empirical science to support the claims they had made about same-sex marriage during the voting campaign, the judge ruled that it was unconstitutional to continue to deny same-sex couples the right to marry. Anti-Prop 8 attorney Theodore B. Olson said, "We did put fear and prejudice on trial, and fear and prejudice lost."

The YouTube video of the play *8*, featuring George Clooney, Chris Colfer, Jamie Lee Curtis, Jane Lynch, Brad Pitt, and Martin Sheen, among others, is a powerful account of the case, framed around the trial's historic closing arguments in June 2010. It provides a fascinating look at what unfolded when the issues and claims surrounding same-sex marriage were examined in depth. The pro–Prop 8/anti-gay marriage forces lost that case, but because they have appealed, same-sex marriage is still illegal in California, pending the ruling on the appeal.

FOUR

THE PRIVILEGE OF FAMILY: JENNIFER CHRISLER INVITES TONY PERKINS TO DINNER

Where you go I will go, and where you stay I will stay. Your
people will be my people and your God my God.
—Ruth 1:16

What gay people long for is to have the same right as straight people to create loving families that are legally recognized everywhere, and accorded the same privileges.

Tony Perkins, president of the Family Research Council, in Washington, D.C., is one of the most vocal and active leaders working to make sure they don't get that recognition or those privileges, even though, as of this writing, he clearly knows almost nothing about gay people or their relationships. That may soon change.

In an interview with CNN Newsroom anchor Brooke Baldwin in May 2012, Perkins admitted that he had never been to the home of a married same-sex couple. She asked him, "If you were ever invited to the home of one of these couples, how would you tell them to their face that their marriage is not valid and yours is?"

Perkins replied that it was not a matter of individual couples and how they would take it personally, but that rather a matter of good public policy. He said that there "might be homosexual couples who make great parents, but that's not what the overwhelming amount of social science says." Baldwin pointed out the obvious to Perkins: "For these couples," she said, "it very much is a matter of individuals, and it's a very personal issue to them." Unfortunately, she didn't get a chance to dispute Perkins' claims about what social science says—or if she did, it was edited out in the CNN program clip.

Jennifer Chrisler, executive director of the Family Equality Council, saw their exchange in the newscast. She and her wife, Cheryl Jacques, are the mothers of twin 10-year-olds and just welcomed a new baby. She sent Perkins an invitation to dinner at her house, care of his Family Research Council.

"As Christians," she wrote, "I think we can both agree that ours is not to judge and that we must live by the golden rule. I open my table to you and invite you to get to know me and my family.

"I, like you, am a parent. Like you, my spouse and I have shared many years together committed to our family, our community, and to making the world a better place," she continued. "I imagine we share many of the same joys and struggles in doing the important work of raising our children and contributing meaningfully to our community. We attend church regularly and our children attend Sunday school weekly. We love our children intensely and feel a deep desire to protect and nurture them as they continue along their journey to adulthood. ... This is the face of the one million families you have taken no time to get to know."

Perkins accepted the invitation and told CNN that he and his wife planned to go as soon as they could find a time that worked for both families.

Chrisler said she was happily surprised that Perkins agreed to visit. "It really incenses me when people like Tony Perkins say all kinds of hateful things about me, my family, my kids, and he doesn't even know who we are," she told Baldwin. "I find that really outrageous, and frankly, so disingenuous on his part.

"I tell my 10-year-olds, if you're having problems with somebody, if you don't understand them and they don't understand you, then talking to each other is the first step."

When Baldwin asked if she thought the dinner would change Perkins' beliefs, Chrisler said that she doubted it, but that she hoped it would "soften his heart."

One of the ways Tony Perkins' Family Research Council fights equal rights for the LGBT community is through active support of the Defense of Marriage Act (DOMA). The Council gives out a free 16-page brochure in support of DOMA that, oddly enough, gives no reasons why allowing same-sex marriages will hurt the institution of marriage. It mainly states the pro- and anti-DOMA legal actions that have occurred and also lists the laws that the Council feels have hurt American morality over time. In truth, DOMA does nothing to hurt traditional marriage, but it does exceptional damage to LGBT couples and their families.

HOW DOMA IS HURTING FAMILIES, ESPECIALLY FAMILIES WITH CHILDREN

In 1996 Congress enacted the Defense of Marriage Act, which defines marriage as the legal union of one man and one woman. Under the law, no state is required to recognize another state's same-sex marriage. In addition, DOMA's Section 3 says that same-sex marriage should not be recognized for any federal purposes, including Social Security survivor's benefits, government employee insurance benefits, and joint tax returns.

DOMA not only penalizes same-sex couples, it also hurts their children by denying them the basic rights and safety nets that children of opposite-sex couples have.

According to the Family Equality Council (FEC), DOMA penalizes the two million U.S. children being raised by LGBT parents today in a variety of ways that force their families to struggle much harder to make ends meet. Here are just a few:

Insurance Employers are not required to extend health insurance benefits to the partners of LGBT employees or to the children of these partners. So families are not covered when the main breadwinner is not allowed to be one of the children's legal parents. They must pay thousands in extra insurance premiums if they want their children covered.

Fewer tax credits and deductions Because the federal government does not recognize LGBT families, it's harder for them to maximize dependency exemptions and deductions. For example, according to the FEC, a same-sex couple raising two children with an income of $45,000 a year would pay $2,165 in taxes annually, while a married heterosexual couple with two children and the same income would receive a $50 refund.

No joint federal tax return Married straight couples usually pay less when filing jointly, but married gay couples don't have that option and end up paying more.

DOMA affects more than just finances, however. If married same-sex couples live in a state that doesn't honor that marriage, all their spousal rights disappear. When Webster Williams suddenly fell ill in 2008, his partner of 26 years, Frank Russo, had the foresight to grab their signed and notarized local domestic partner registration and health-care proxy legal forms before they went to the nearby emergency room. Russo wanted to be there to support him and figured the paperwork would prevent any "not a family member" problems.

When Williams was admitted and taken in to see a doctor, however, the guard would not allow Russo to accompany him—in spite of the paperwork. Fortunately, Williams was still conscious and able to tell a nurse the problem. The nurse made arrangements for Russo to enter the emergency room and apologized. If Williams had been unconscious, however, or the nurse had been as intransigent as the guard, his partner would have had to begin proceedings with the hospital administration. Worse yet, if the incident had happened when they were out of town, in a hospital that didn't honor their home state's legal paperwork, Russo would have had to contact Williams' out-of-state family simply to get the hospital to give out any information on his status. This is unconscionable by almost anyone's standards.

In 2011 the Obama administration announced that DOMA's Section 3 was unconstitutional and that although the administration would continue to enforce the law, it would no longer defend it in court. In response, the House of Representatives has undertaken the law's defense. Several court challenges at the state level have also found DOMA's Section 3 to be unconstitutional, so it will eventually make its way to the Supreme Court.

FIVE

WHAT THE BIBLE SAYS

Now these three remain: faith, hope, and love.
But the greatest of these is love.
–1 Corinthians 13:13

There are more than 2,000 Bible verses that describe God's immense concern and love for the poor and the oppressed, and very few that deal with homosexuality. But in a world full of poverty, disasters, and injustice, some Christians focus instead on lobbying for laws that legalize discrimination against gay people–many of whom surely fit into the category of oppressed. This flies in the face of the gospel love for our neighbors that Jesus preached.

Homosexual is not a word that is used anywhere in the Bible, even though historic evidence points to the fact that homosexuality has always been around and was practiced openly and widely in the Greek and Roman cultures that were dominant in New Testament times. In Chapter 3 under Myth 5, we have already examined the Genesis account of Adam and Eve. Here we look at the few additional biblical passages that deal with issues concerning homosexuality.

OLD TESTAMENT

Genesis 19:1–14 The term sodomy came from this passage, which recounts the story of the men of Sodom who demanded that Lot present his guests—angels disguised as mortal men—so that they could gang rape them. This story says nothing about homosexual attraction and love, but clearly imputes evil to the crimes of rape (a crime of violence, motivated by hostility and a need to exercise power, not by sexual desire) and inhospitality to travelers.

* * *

Leviticus 18:22 and 20:13 These verses say that men who have intercourse with men are an abomination and (in 20:13) ought to be stoned to death. The verses are part of ancient Israel's holiness code, detailed in various sections of the first five books of the Old Testament. The code also commands death by stoning for people who work on the Sabbath and for stubborn and rebellious sons, adulterers, and a host of other lawbreakers. It declares the following practices taboo and/or abominations: getting a tattoo, planting two kinds of seed in one field, having any physical contact with women during their menstruation, wearing clothes with mixed fabrics, and eating shellfish. Many of these "abominations" require the death sentence. Selling your daughter into slavery, however, or buying slaves from neighboring countries, was perfectly legitimate. Clearly this was a different era.

How Did Stigmas Against Male Homosexuality Come About in the First Place?

In ancient times, life was hard, and chances were high that nomadic tribes such as the Israelites could be wiped out by disease, natural disasters, battles, and other calamities. The tribe's survival, therefore, depending on having as high a birthrate as possible. People believed that the seed (semen) of a male was the only thing that created life. They weren't aware that the semen fertilized an egg, and that the female reproductive system played an equal role in conception. So anything that wasted seed was taboo. Men were considered defiled if they had nocturnal emissions (dreams with erotic images that cause an orgasm while the male is asleep), if they masturbated, or if they had intercourse with another man, because they were wasting seed that could have been used to impregnate a wife or concubine.[11] Although lesbian behavior also occurred, it was never addressed, because it played no role in wasting "the seed of life."

NEW TESTAMENT
JESUS IN THE GOSPELS

By the time of the New Testament, homosexuality was widespread among the Greeks and Romans. The Greeks in particular believed that women were inferior to men, and that belief made them value homosexual love more than heterosexual love. Greek philosophers often called it the best kind of love. Although he surely must have been aware of this viewpoint, Jesus never addressed homosexuality or anything that could be remotely construed as homosexuality, even in Matthew 15:18,19, when he defined a list of sins similar to those of Paul in 1 Corinthians 6:9–10 and 1 Timothy 1:9–10. He never said homosexuality was a sin, in spite of the fact that the Old Testament system for maintaining purity was upheld and practiced among devout Jews of his time, in contrast to the practices of the dominant Greco-Roman culture.

Under that system, your holiness and purity depended not only on your practice, but also on your family, your physical condition, your economic class, and your gender. Priests and members of the tribe of Levi (Levites) were considered the most pure, followed by men who were born Jewish, followed by converts, followed by bastards, followed by men who weren't "whole": those with damaged or missing limbs, the chronically ill (including those with leprosy), men who slept with men, eunuchs, and men with damaged testicles or penises.

If you touched someone or something impure you became impure also until you performed certain bathing rituals and sacrificial offerings, depending on the level of the impurity. And even if you were born into the right kind of family, if you were too poor to be able to obey all of the laws and comply with the requirements for sacrifice, you were also impure.

These were the rules governing male purity; there were similar rules for women, with a menstruating woman being particularly taboo. A woman suffering from chronic menstruation would therefore be chronically untouchable.

Jesus' approach to these sharp social boundaries was, "Be compassionate as God is compassionate" (Luke 6:36), rather than "Be holy as God is holy," an exhortation stated repeatedly in Leviticus. The only time Jesus said, "Be perfect as God is perfect" (Matthew 5:48), he first completely redefined the definition of perfection (Matthew 5:43-47) as loving your enemies as well as your neighbors, a radical concept for the people of that era.

Jesus attacked those who fulfilled the letter of the law without fulfilling its spirit. His parables were peopled with those outside the Jewish establishment: the Good Samaritan, widows, the poor, unfortunates, and even the unclean were the heroes. He consorted with "tax collectors and sinners," and often shared meals with men and women who were considered defiled—something no Pharisee in good standing would even contemplate. He laid his healing hands upon lepers, women with discharges, and other untouchables.

A big part of the good news that Jesus proclaimed was a kingdom of Heaven with an open table that welcomed all comers. So it's ironic that traditional Christians who claim to follow Jesus' teaching would want to deny the LGBT community access to Christ's communion.

SELECTIVE BIBLICAL LITERALISM IS HYPOCRISY

Jesus never speaks against homosexuality, but he does speak very clearly against divorce and remarriage. Yet the majority of churches today—including those who view non-celibate homosexuals as sinners—not only accept divorced members, including those who have remarried, but also allow them to be church leaders.

There are cultural justifications for that: Marriage was a different institution in the time of Jesus, and divorce was so biased in favor of men that it could result in financial devastation, loss of children, and many other unjust consequences for women. So making cultural allowances for modern divorce seems fair—clearly it was a different issue in ancient cultures. So why do we not make the same cultural allowance for modern gay unions, giving those couples the same acceptance enjoyed by the heterosexuals whom Jesus actually classified as sinners?

This selective literalism in both the Old and New Testament is unjust. It defies the most universal of Christ's commandments, the one whose meaning no stretch of time or evolution in culture or history can change: the Golden Rule.

THE FIRST U.S. PRESIDENT TO ENDORSE SAME-SEX MARRIAGE

In May 2012, President Barack Obama made history as the first U.S. president to publicly support same-sex marriage. When he explained his new position to ABC reporter Robin Roberts, he mentioned conversations with "friends and family and neighbors" and with his daughters who have friends with same-sex parents. He spoke about gay members of his own staff "in incredibly committed monogamous relationships." And he talked about how knowing those people and having those talks prompted him to change his views on same-sex marriage, just like a lot of other Americans. He also pointed out that he and his wife are both practicing Christians, and this was a matter of the Golden Rule: "You know, treat others the way you would want to be treated."

His declaration reflected the amazing pace of change in American opinion on an issue that seemed almost immovable before. As recently as 2004, a Pew Research Center poll found that 60 percent of Americans were opposed to allowing same-sex couples to marry, with 36 percent strongly opposed. In April 2012, just before President Obama's announcement, however, the opposition had decreased to 43 percent, with 22 percent strongly opposed.

Clearly, a fresh observance of the Golden Rule is at work here. A majority of Americans now recognize that gay people deserve the same opportunities for love and commitment as straight people. And many Christians no longer believe there is any biblical reason for denying them those civil rights.

To return to our New Testament survey, there are only three short passages in the New Testament that have traditionally been considered anti-gay. We'll examine each of them to show that, given current biblical scholarship, that view is no longer tenable, and that it contradicts the basic principles of the message of Jesus. Not only that, but the New Testament passage describing the first gentile to become a Christian reinforces the message that the holiness codes must be set aside to make way for the love of Jesus.

* * *

Acts 8:26–40 It is significant that the first gentile (non-Jew) to become a Christian in the New Testament was an Ethiopian eunuch. Here was a man who, according to Old Testament law, was not only a gentile, but also unclean, someone who had been castrated. Yet according to Acts, God sent an angel to tell Philip to go share the Gospel with this seeker (who, in turn, chose to be baptized immediately), making it very clear that this was God's wish, not a fluke of Philip's travels.

* * *

Romans 1:23–27 In these verses, Paul writes about women and men who "exchange natural relations for unnatural relations" with people of the same gender. He calls it shameful, and in context he is clearly referring to people who are worshiping idols. Paul wrote to the Romans from Corinth, where Aphrodite was worshiped. Her temple had the images of "mortal men, birds, animals, and reptiles," which Paul describes in verse 23. Like some of the other religious sects of that era, the worship of Aphrodite involved temple prostitution, including male prostitutes who were known for their debauchery.

Many traditional Christians claim that Paul also believed that homosexuality itself was unnatural. He very well could have, just as he likely believed other health myths of that era, such as the assumption that epilepsy was caused by demonic possession (Matthew 17:15–21). We know today that epilepsy is caused by an imbalance in brain chemistry or brain damage, not demons. We also know that homosexuality is not unnatural, although it is a trait manifested by a minority of the population, like left-handedness. Therefore, gay Christians in faithful, loving relationships are engaging in natural behavior, behavior that would not be included in Paul's condemnations. What is unnatural and unhealthy, in fact, is trying to force gay people to engage in heterosexual relationships or else to be celibate for life in order to be accepted at Christ's table.

Dennis R. MacDonald, John Wesley Professor of New Testament and Christian Origins at Claremont School of Theology in California, also points out that the ancients did not have the understanding of homosexuality that we do today. We now know that some people have an innate attraction to the same sex. However, the Greco-Roman thinking during the era of Jesus was that men were capable of sexually enjoying both men and women, and they would pursue whichever they enjoyed the most. Often, says MacDonald, this meant that powerful men forced boys (who were frequently slaves) to gratify their sexual urges, behave like girls, and submit to other exploitive demands. Some boys were even castrated to preserve their youthful qualities. If Paul frowned upon such practices, it's perfectly understandable. So would we. There's a world of difference between coercion and mutual love, between exploitation and partnership.

* * *

1 Corinthians 6:9–10, 1 Timothy 1:9–10 Both of these passages list the kinds of sinners who will not inherit the kingdom of God: fornicators, idolaters, adulterers, drunkards, and
murderers. The Corinthians passage adds two more: in the
original Greek, *malakoi* and *arsenokoitai.* Timothy adds only
arsenokoitai.

Numerous Bible scholars, both liberal and conservative,
point out that Paul's terms were not standard Greek words for
homosexual behavior, which would imply that he was not
referring to homosexuals in general. There's been quite a bit
of scholarly debate as to how to translate these words.
Translations differ radically in the various versions of the
Bible, including the New International, King James, Revised
Standard, and Modern Language. The Bibles that translate
one or the other of these words as "homosexuals" or "practicing homosexuals," reflect the bias of the translators rather
than the literal Greek meanings.

The first word, *malakoi,* means people who are "soft" and is
an extremely common Greek word both in the New
Testament and in Greek literature. Its connotations include
people who are "sick," "cowardly," "refined," "weak-willed,"
"delicate," and/or "gentle." In a moral context it frequently

means people who are "debauched," "loose," "wanton," or "lacking self-control" and never refers to gay people as a group, but rather to heterosexual people or activities. However, in a few references it refers to young men who hire themselves out to play the passive role in a same-sex relationship. That is why *malakoi* is often translated as "homosexual prostitute," although it could just as easily be translated "wanton."

Arsenokoitai is more difficult to translate because it is quite rare. It literally means "male" and "intercourse." It used to be translated as "masturbators," but by the twentieth century masturbation had become a more generally accepted behavior, and so scholars looked for other possible translations. Those who believe homosexuality is a sin tend to translate it as "practicing homosexuals." But many scholars now believe it means "males who have intercourse" and refers specifically to male prostitutes who serve both males and females—especially since the word was used for *qadesh*, the Hebrew word for male temple prostitute, in early Greek translations of 1 Kings 14:24, 15:12 and 22:46. (The King James Version and other older English versions of the Bible translate *qadesh* as "sodomite." Both liberal and conservative Bible scholars agree, however, that the Hebrew word *qadesh* means male temple or cult prostitutes.) On one point the scholars are unanimous: No one can be absolutely certain about the definition of *arsenokoitai*.

Obviously, these verses are very dubious grounds for declaring homosexuality in general to be a sin.

A POSTSCRIPT, IN MEMORY OF GARY

In the course of writing the above summary of biblical scholarship on the subject of homosexuality, I interviewed both conservative evangelical and progressive New Testament Greek professors for fact checking.

The evangelical professor I interviewed recommended that I read *The Moral Vision of the New Testament*, by Richard B. Hays. I thought the chapter on homosexuality in this book had many problems with logic, but I mention it here because Hays cited a friend of his named Gary who had recently died of AIDS. Gary believed that homosexuality was a sin, and had struggled his whole life with it. He strongly believed his homosexuality hindered his ability to serve God. Hays writes as if Gary's views bolstered his case against homosexuality, but in my view, they are a tragic but perfect example of what is wrong with these views.

If homosexuality had been accepted in Gary's church and monogamous gay relationships encouraged as much as monogamous straight ones, Gary–clearly a devout seeker who didn't have the gift for celibacy–might have found a life partner. He certainly would not have believed that his natural desires were sinful. The support of a loving partner and the lack of self-hatred would have enabled him to better use his gifts for ministry in the church, and he would have been far less likely to have engaged in clandestine sexual encounters and contracted HIV. Instead of spending so much energy struggling with a nature that was God-given, Gary could have served God as he wished–and lived.

IF THIS "NEW" INTERPRETATION OF THE BIBLE IS TRUE, HOW COULD CHRISTIANS HAVE HAD IT WRONG ALL THESE YEARS?

Throughout history, there have been many mainstream Christian beliefs that have been proven dead wrong. Often these beliefs lasted hundreds of years and formed the basis for institutions and actions that were anything but Christian. The most commonly cited examples are the Inquisition and the Crusades, but more recent history has also had its share. For many centuries, good Christians used the Bible as a basis to deny women basic human and civil rights, such as inheritance and property ownership; to imply that handicapped people must have sinned to deserve their disability, and to justify anti-Semitism. In the United States, in the early 1900s, conservative Christian churches were the main opponents of women's suffrage (the right to vote).

Since so many Bible verses seemed to allow for slavery, it wasn't until the late 1700s that Christians began seriously questioning its morality. When the United States finally abolished slavery in 1865, many sincere Christians still believed it was a valid state for black people. There were two biblical "justifications" they cited: Some believed Africans bore the mark of Cain, whom God cursed for killing his brother, and others believed that Africans were Hamites: Ham mocked his father Noah, who cursed Ham's descendants, saying they would be slaves to the descendants of his brothers. Because of such beliefs, some Christian colleges in the South continued to bar blacks from attending through the 1960s and 1970s.

Interracial dating was considered sinful for many years because of certain Bible verses. It wasn't until 1967 that the U.S. Supreme Court struck down the last of the state laws banning interracial marriage, and Christian college Bob Jones University did not lift its ban against interracial dating until March 2000.

History has shown that harmful beliefs continue until people begin to question them, even in the church. And the questioning is always controversial at first. Traditions, even negative ones, die hard. We didn't begin questioning society's prejudice against homosexuality until UCLA psychologist Evelyn Hooker first began examining it in the 1950s (see Chapter 6), so it's not surprising that it is still controversial.

* * *

There are only three verses that deal with homosexuality in the New Testament, and the majority of New Testament Greek scholars would argue that those three verses don't deal with homosexuality as we define it today, but rather with temple prostitution and other abuses. Although Jesus must have been familiar with the homosexual practices in society, he says nothing about them, other than what can be inferred from his example of loving and accepting everyone, even those whom the religious establishment considered unclean.

If the church thoughtfully and prayerfully confronts the evidence and issues, it's only a matter of time before it embraces the love and acceptance of LGBT people that Christ has meant us to have all along.

SIX

Is It Really a Choice?

Before I formed you in the womb, I knew you.

—Jeremiah 1:5

The fact that I'm heterosexual didn't come as a gradual awakening or a sudden revelation, and it certainly wasn't a conscious choice. It was just something I always was. I didn't think much about it until the late 1980s when I started getting to know gay men and lesbians who were beginning to dare to come out. For them, there was a moment in their childhood or adolescence when they realized that who they were was not officially acceptable and that they had better keep quiet about it. They considered the idea that they would choose to be that way ludicrous.

"Why would I choose an identity that society thinks is evil, that I will be teased and taunted and maybe even murdered for, and that my church tells me will send me straight to hell?" they would ask. "It would be so much easier if I could choose to be straight."

My church, however, told me their homosexuality was a choice. So I wondered, could I, a life-long heterosexual, choose to be gay, even for five minutes? It seemed insane, but since my church assured me it was possible, I decided to try fantasizing about various women I admired to see if I could manufacture homosexual feelings by choice. I could not. This simply reinforced the belief I now shared with my gay friends—that sexual orientation wasn't a matter of choice but a matter of nature.

I suspect that the myth of choice came about because of people who are truly bisexual, or "fluid." Current studies suggest that 2.8 to 6 percent of males and 1 to 4 percent of females are homosexual, and perhaps as many as 30 percent of all people are fluid. Estimates of the bisexual percentage vary widely, however, depending on how bisexuality is defined. But I have never met anyone, gay, straight, or bi, who thought that his or her original orientation was a choice. I've only met those struggling to choose to change.

In many places today, being gay still means:

• You must not fall in love, by the law of your church

• You may not marry, by the law of your state

• You may suffer verbal abuse and physical harm

• You may be fired from your job

• You may be murdered

• You may be rejected by friends, neighbors, and family

• You may be declared unfit to raise children

• You may be excommunicated from your church and/or
condemned to hell

So why would people in those places *choose* to be gay?

Modern science didn't begin to investigate these issues until
the 1950s. At that time, psychologist Evelyn Hooker decided
to begin research into sexual orientation after she got to know
a gay student who attended one of her classes at UCLA. He
didn't fit any of the era's negative stereotypes of a homosexual. She published the results of her research in 1957, con-
cluding that "homosexuals were not inherently abnormal and
that there was no difference between homosexual and heterosexual men in terms of pathology."

There have been many studies since then, and in 1973, the American Psychiatric Association deleted homosexuality from the list of sexual deviances in its *Diagnostic and Statistical Manual of Mental Disorders.*

In 1999, the American Academy of Pediatrics, the American Counseling Association, the American Association of School Administrators, the American Federation of Teachers, the American Psychiatric Association, the American Psychological Association, the American School Health Association, the Interfaith Alliance Foundation, the National Association of School Psychologists, the National Association of Social Workers and the National Education Association jointly issued a statement in a publication titled "Just the Facts About Sexual Orientation & Youth: A Primer for Principals, Educators and School Personnel" that said, "Homosexuality is not a mental disorder and thus there is no need for a 'cure' ... Health and mental health professional organizations do not support efforts to change young people's sexual orientation through 'reparative therapy' and have raised serious concerns about its potential to do harm."

A similar and even larger group of respected experts issued an update of the same publication in 2008, with the same message, adding that those who engage in "reparative therapy" had "serious potential to harm young people because they present the view that the sexual orientation of lesbian, gay, and bisexual youth is a mental illness or disorder, and they often frame the inability to change one's sexual orientation as a personal and moral failure."

Today *all* major professional medical and scientific organizations believe that a person's sexual orientation is not a choice and that it is almost impossible to change.

In the past couple of decades, science has begun investigating possible biological reasons for homosexuality. The August 30, 1991 issue of *Science* magazine published a paper by Simon LeVay, Ph.D., on the differences he had discovered between the brain structures of gay and straight deceased men. Similar studies followed. Since about 8 percent of sheep are homosexual, endocrinologists did a study that compared the brains of rams that consistently preferred males with those that preferred females. The February 2004 issue of the journal *Endocrinology* reported their results: the differences between the brains of the homosexual and heterosexual sheep were similar to what LeVay had found in humans.

What causes a person to develop a particular sexual orientation, however—whether heterosexual, homosexual, or bisexual—is still unclear. Scientists suspect the causes are mostly genetic and hormonal, but no one knows for sure. However, the pre-1950s view that your after-birth environment and culture alone determine your sexual orientation is no longer held by any major professional or scientific organization.

Now that there is less stigma surrounding homosexuality in some cities, one or two radical gay groups have begun encouraging people to choose to be gay. This is as ridiculous as choosing to be straight, of course. If you have a choice, you are bisexual. You can choose to date only people of the same sex if you buy into these groups' reasoning, but that doesn't mean you'll become homosexual. You'll still be bisexual.

Do Gay Animals Have a Choice?

The question is a joke, obviously, but many people don't realize that homosexuality also commonly occurs in animals. The percentage of gay behavior varies from species to species. Bonobo chimpanzees are the most fluid, and bisexual behavior is an absolute necessity within their social structure. They reduce stress and work out problems by having frequent intercourse with other members of their group, no matter what their sex. Many other animals have homosexuality and bisexuality rates similar to those of humans.[12]

There are also billions of animals and plants that are literally bisexual: creatures that can change sexes or be both sexes simultaneously because they have both male and female reproductive organs. These are called hermaphrodites. Many fish, and almost all snails and slugs, earthworms, and the vast majority of plants are hermaphrodites.

I IS FOR INTERSEX, Q IS FOR QUEER OR QUESTIONING

Hermaphrodites are much rarer among humans and mammals. Today the term intersex is the preferred usage for humans with male and female genitalia and/or chromosomes, since the word hermaphrodite can be considered negative. It is also too limited to describe the different sexual variations with which intersex people are born. That's why you will sometimes see the abbreviation "LGBTI," with "I" added to include intersex, acknowledging a difference between intersex and transgender people. You will also see LGBTIQ, with "Q" or even "QQ" added for queer or questioning: an umbrella term for anything that the other initials don't cover. Today, many younger LGBT people refer to themselves as queer as a way of taking a formerly pejorative term and using it with pride.

In former times, if a child was born with both male and female genitalia, the doctors encouraged the parents to pick a sex and surgically remove the genitalia that didn't agree with the choice. As these children grew up, however, a significant number had strong gender identities that were the opposite of the one their parents had chosen. Obviously, that was extremely traumatic since they no longer had the correct organs for their natural gender.

Now pediatricians recommend that intersex newborns be given hormone and other tests to determine which gender is most likely to be dominant. Then they suggest the parents name and raise the child in that gender (or pick a gender if neither seems to be dominant), but leave all the child's organs intact. Once the child reaches adolescence, he or she can affirm or change the parents' gender choice, and decide whether to keep both sets of genitalia or go through an operation to remove one set. (See Appendix B, "Transgender and Intersex Communities" for more information.)

SEVEN

WHAT ABOUT "EX-GAYS"?

> For you created my inmost being; you knit me
> together in my mother's womb.
> —Psalm 139:13

The worst thing about "ex-gay" groups is that their existence causes well-meaning and loving Christians to continue to stigmatize homosexuality and drive vulnerable young people away from their churches. That's because when church youth admit they are struggling with same-sex attraction, their pastors and parents often encourage them to connect with an ex-gay group so they can "choose" to become straight. Problem solved. Then, when these idealistic young Christians discover that the ex-gay groups don't work and come back to their church to explain, their church penalizes them.

"Other Christians have successfully become ex-gay; you must not be trusting Jesus enough," they are often told. The only trouble is, other Christians have not managed to become ex-gay. They never have.

Michael Bussee was one of the original founders of what is now Exodus International, the world's largest and best-known Christian organization that, until recently, claimed to help people become ex-gay. He is now convinced and very articulate about why ex-gay organizations do serious harm to many vulnerable people. His own story, which he recounted to me in an in-depth phone interview in 1994, is a case in point.[13]

As a young person, Bussee knew he was supposed to fall in love with a woman—any woman—and he tried his best to do so. He prayed. He underwent therapy. He got married. He even got a master's degree in counseling. None of that stopped him from being attracted to men.

While Bussee was pursuing his psychology studies, someone told him that even though he felt homosexual attraction, because he was a Christian he was not homosexual. Rather, he was a "former homosexual" who would grow into his true identity. God would bless his faithfulness by gradually replacing his homosexual feelings with heterosexual ones.

This was a tremendous relief to Bussee, and he started teaching a seminar on how gay people could become heterosexual. It was the beginning of what would become Exodus.

Bussee lectured all over the country on how Jesus was healing his homosexuality. He counseled hundreds of people. In the process, he met another counselor, Gary Cooper, and that's when things started getting complicated. They tried to hide from themselves and each other that they were in love. At the same time they began to notice something.

After one or two years in the Exodus program, people who had initially responded with a lot of hope were becoming extremely depressed because they were not changing. "One of the very harmful things that these programs [were telling you at that time]," said Bussee, "is that if you don't change, you're not doing enough, you don't have enough faith. An increasing number of them became self-destructive. One man slashed his genitals and poured Drano on them."

Busee and Cooper eventually admitted that Exodus wasn't working for the people they were counseling any more than it was working for themselves. They divorced their wives and married each other in 1979. After much study, said Bussee, they had come to believe that homosexuality, like heterosexuality, was morally neutral in God's eyes.

Because there is a spectrum of gay, bisexual, and straight orientation, highly motivated gay men and lesbians who are at least a little bisexual can manage to "go straight" for a time and even marry and engage in sexual relations with their spouses, although such marriages usually don't last. Gay men and lesbians may fantasize that they are making love to a person of the same sex in order to reach orgasm and conceive children with their spouses. Even though their feelings, fantasies, and self-identification remain homosexual, people like these are often cited as ex-gay success stories.

Going straight is not quite as difficult for highly motivated bisexuals who lean toward homosexuality but want to change. However, all major mental health professional organizations point to the overwhelming evidence that actual "cures," where truly gay people replace their homosexual feelings with heterosexual feelings for the rest of their lives and genuinely become ex-gay, are impossible to sustain for the long term, and usually have harmful consequences when attempted.

Fortunately, the Exodus International website no longer claims that it can help people become ex-gay, although many other similar groups still make such claims. In a June 26, 2012 Associated Press article by Patrick Condon that was picked up by media outlets throughout the nation, Alan Chambers, the current president of Exodus International, admitted that he no longer uses the term ex-gay because he still struggles with his own homosexuality, in spite of his marriage to an understanding woman, with whom he has children.

Based on the fact that the vast majority of Exodus members

admit to the same struggles, he is leading Exodus away from the idea that gay people's sexual orientation can be changed or "cured." According to the article, Chambers has recently deleted books endorsing ex-gay therapy from the Exodus online bookstore and is encouraging member ministries to cease promoting such therapy.

Furthermore, the Exodus website no longer includes a FAQ speculating about what percentage of gay people may be able to go straight. The last I checked, it had an article titled "Big Foot, Nessie & Exodus International" by its former public relations director, Julie Neils, ending with this paragraph:

"Exodus International doesn't exist to make gay people straight, promote a formula for 'success,' to make money, or even to pass legislation. We exist to help others live a life that reflects the Christian faith. We've found that the opposite of homosexuality is most certainly not heterosexuality. It is holiness. It is loving God and being loved by Him. It is accepting His identity for us, instead of everyone else's."

"YOU MUST REMAIN CELIBATE IN ORDER TO BE TRULY CHRISTIAN."

Julie Neils is reflecting what many traditional Christians, gay

as well as straight, believe: that same-gender sexual intercourse is not permissible for practicing Christians. Since they
can't be "cured," God must want them to be celibate.

So now straight traditional Christians who are married
(even divorcees who are remarried) feel they are being open-
minded when they admit that homosexuals can't change their
nature, so therefore they are willing to welcome them as fellow Christians as long as they strive for celibacy. In other
words, it's OK for straight people to ask gay people to be celibate, even though they do not require it of themselves. But
would a just and loving God who said it is not good for people to be alone make an exception of LGBT people?

Some Christian leaders go so far as to say that for secular
justice to prevail, the government should get out of the busi-
ness of marrying people and only give legal status to civil
unions, leaving marriage as a sacred institution for the
church. Although it's wonderful that they admit it's a matter
of justice for the LGBT community to have partnership rights
in society, we call these partnerships marriages. How, then,
can it not be a matter of justice in the church too? In civil
society, these leaders advocate for justice and love; in the
church, they cling to highly questionable translations of a few
Bible verses, and thus perpetuate second-class citizenship for

the LGBT community and continuing stigmatism and oppression for them in Christianity.

"WE'RE ONLY TRYING TO HELP GAYS AND LESBIANS WHO WANT TO BECOME STRAIGHT."

Although Exodus no longer supports ex-gay therapy, other prominent conservative Christian groups like Focus on the Family still do, arguing that they're actually doing gay people a loving service—they're just trying to help homosexuals who want to become straight. They ignore the fact that the reason these people are so motivated to struggle against their God-given nature is because of the preaching of groups like theirs.

Nobel laureate Archbishop Desmond Tutu has pointed out that it's just as absurd for black people to wish they were white as it is for gay people to wish they were straight. In his long struggle against apartheid in South Africa, he met many black people who wished they could be white. The problem wasn't that blacks were inferior to whites but that apartheid treated them as if they were. And the solution wasn't to turn their skins a different color, but to change society to accept all colors equally. It's the same for gay people: instead of requiring them to try to become straight to fit in, society must accept them for who they are.

EIGHT

CONCLUSION: START THE HEALING

But Jacob replied, "I will not let you go unless you bless me."
—Genesis 32:26

When traditional beliefs are clearly causing hurt instead of blessing, it's worth struggling with the issues involved in order to come out on the other side, just as Jacob struggled with the angel of the Lord. In this case the struggle means taking the courageous step of letting go of harmful traditional beliefs so we can embrace the blessing reflected in the compassion of Jesus.

There is no scientific or ethical reason and no good religious reason to define homosexuality as immoral. For Christians to continue to insist that it is wrong is to do grave injustice in the name of Jesus to some of society's most vulnerable people. It's time to apologize for the years of hurtful slander, condemnation, and persecution of the LGBT community.

Christians must cease instilling self-loathing in gay young people. Stop telling gay people it's against their religion to fall in love and marry. Stop telling those whom God has called to the ministry that they aren't even worthy to sit at Christ's table. It's time to stop persecuting gay people. It's time to accept them as the equal members of God's family that they are. It's time to start the healing.

APPENDICES

(All Internet web addresses cited are accurate as of September 2012.)

A. FOR MORE INFORMATION AND SUPPORT

This book only summarizes LGBT (lesbian, gay, bisexual, and transgender) issues. There are many excellent resources for those seeking an in-depth look at the concerns it covers. One of the best books that I've read, especially for those from an evangelical background, just came out: Justin Lee's *Torn: Rescuing the Gospel from the Gays vs. Christians Debate.*

Other helpful books include *God vs. Gay? The Religious Case for Equality*, by Jay Michaelson, which covers other religions in addition to Christianity; *Is the Homosexual My Neighbor? Revised and Updated: A Positive Christian Response*, by Letha Dawson Scanzoni and Virginia Ramey Mollenkott; *What God Has Joined Together: The Christian Case for Gay Marriage* by David G. Myers and Letha Dawson Scanzoni; *Jesus, the Bible, and Homosexuality*, by Presbyterian theologian Jack Rogers; *What the Bible Really Says About Homosexuality*, by Roman Catholic priest and theologian Daniel A. Helminiak; and the 1994 classic, *Stranger at the Gate: To be Gay and Christian in*

America, by Mel White, pastor and former ghost writer for Pat Robertson, Jerry Falwell, and other national evangelists. The website www.religioustolerance.org is also useful for explaining Bible references from all points of view (traditional included), with references.

The Trevor Project, www.thetrevorproject.org, is an admirable national organization that provides crisis intervention and suicide prevention services to LGBT youth and adults. Its lifeline, 866-4-U-TREVOR (866-488-7386), is open 24 hours a day.

If you are a family member or friend of an LGBT person and looking for information and help, PFLAG.org (Parents, Families, and Friends of Lesbians and Gays) is what you need.

The Gay Christian Network (www.gaychristian.net) is a wonderful networking and support group for gay Christians, especially those who are struggling with traditional Christian views. There are also helpful LGBT websites for almost every religious denomination, even denominations that are not officially supportive. You can find them by Googling the word *gay* along with the denomination (for example Dignity USA, the site for LGBT Catholics, is found by Googling *gay Catholics*, and OrthoGays, the site for religiously observant gay Jews, is found by Googling *gay Orthodox Jews*). These organizations often offer valuable resources, including study guides and videos, for individuals and groups who are beginning the journey toward becoming more LGBT friendly and inclusive. This book, of course, can also be used as an introduction to the issues for study groups.

At the beginning of the LGBT civil rights era, many of the activist and support organizations seemed to be predominantly white. Now, however, LGBT organizations for African American, Latino, Asian and other ethnic groups have also come into their own, along with significant conferences for networking, such as the National Queer People of Color Conference, www.qpocc2012.org, which brings LGBT African Americans and Latinos together each spring. Again, you can find such organizations by Googling the word *gay* or *queer* and the ethnicity.

The Gay-Straight Alliance Network, www.gsanetwork.org, is a helpful national organization for students who want to join together to make their school safer and more welcoming for the LGBT community, as well as to network with Gay-Straight Alliance chapters at other schools. Such groups can make a significant difference in the atmosphere of a campus.

Last but not least, there are now many, many role models in the media, including on the Internet, working to help

LGBT young people know they're not alone. One of the best sites created for those who are being persecuted is the "It Gets Better" project, www.itgetsbetter.org. There, religious leaders like Gene Robinson assure LGBT youth that God loves them just as they are and that it really does get better. More than half a million other people, too, have posted videos assuring them that it's worth hanging in there because things won't always be so grim. Such support can be a tremendous source of hope, especially for teens with little or no local support.

Celebrities like Ellen, Anderson Cooper, and Rachel Maddow demonstrate that it's possible to be out and be wildly successful. Even comic books have gay celebrities now— one of the new DC Comics Green Lantern superheroes is gay, for example, and the January 2012 issue of Archie Comics celebrated the wedding of soldier Kevin Keller and Clay Walker, the doctor who took care of Kevin when he was injured in Iraq.

If you have a friend who needs to be broken in to the idea of gay people gradually, *Will & Grace*, one of the first TV comedy series with a gay main character to have widespread popular appeal, is still in reruns and a fun way to begin.

The TV show *Glee* addresses major gay high school issues openly, and usually resolves them in very satisfactory ways.

Those happy endings may not always be realistic; but dreams are often the forerunners of reality.

Broadway and Hollywood have been including compelling gay characters in their plays, documentaries, and movies for years. Many of the films are outstanding. Parents who are having trouble accepting a child's decision to come out, for example, may find comfort and insight in the wonderful 2007 documentary *For the Bible Tells Me So*, by Daniel Karslake, with Nancy Kennedy and Helen R. Mendoza. It vividly recounts the story of five Christian couples—including the parents of Bishop Gene Robinson—coming to terms with their children's homosexuality. For the most recent LGBT-friendly movies, news stories, and other media, check out the GLAAD (Gay & Lesbian Alliance Against Defamation) Media Awards at www.glaad.org.

Those of you who are searching for support and only finding oppression in your local church may very well need to tell them goodbye for your own spiritual and mental health; but don't write off Christianity as a whole quite yet. As I said in Chapter 1: Top Bible scholars, an ever-growing number of denominations, and an even larger number of individual churches are saying, "This we believe: God loves the LGBT community just as much as the straight community and wants LGBT people to have the same rights and opportunities that straight people do, both in the church and in the world." There are millions of us out here. Make sure you find the support you need. The sooner you begin, the better!

B. TRANSGENDER AND INTERSEX COMMUNITIES

Transgender is a broad term that includes anyone who grew up feeling that the sex he or she was born with or assigned at birth was the wrong one. Intersex people–that is, people who were born with both male and female sex organs, ambiguous sex organs, or chromosomes from both sexes–are often included in the transgender category. Some argue, however, that transgender should include only those intersex people who were assigned the wrong gender at birth.

Transgender also refers to anyone who dresses and lives as a member of the opposite sex or dreams about making the change, as well as those who have undergone partial or complete medical transformations to adopt the physical attributes of a different gender.

Their issues are unique and important enough to deserve a book of their own, and fortunately, there are many such books available. For a good reading list and other helpful information, including pointers on how to come out as transgender, see the Human Rights Campaign's transgender sections (go to www.hrc.org, and enter *transgender* in the search section). You can also peruse online bookstores and the many helpful resources on the Internet, including the Intersex Society of North America at www.isna.org and the National Center for Transgender Equality at http://transequality.org, as well as the resources within the various denominational groups mentioned above.

C. ENDNOTES

Chapter 2

1. *Prayers for Bobby: A Mother's Coming to Terms with the Suicide of Her Gay Son*, by Leroy Aarons. New York, NY: HarperCollins Publishers. (A television movie titled *Prayers for Bobby* based on this book premiered on Lifetime in January 2009.)

2. Gay, lesbian, and bisexual adolescents are two* to seven times more likely to attempt suicide and are two to four times more likely to be threatened with a weapon at school, according to "Sexual Orientation and Adolescents" by Barbara L. Frankowski, MD, MPH, the American Academy of Pediatrics Committee on Adolescence, *Pediatrics*, Vol. 113, No. 6, June 2004.

*Every other study I read listed suicide rates as three times or more, including the U.S. Surgeon General's Report and other articles by American Academy of Pediatrics Committee on Adolescence in issues of *Pediatrics*, so I used the larger figure in my text.

3. E. J. Khantzian, M.D. "The self-medication hypothesis of substance use disorders: A reconsideration and recent applications," *Harvard Review of Psychiatry*, January/February 1997.

4. Mark Hatzenbuehler, Ph.D., "The Social Environment and Suicide Attempts in Lesbian, Gay, and Bisexual Youth," *Pediatrics* (the *Journal of the American Academy of Pediatrics*), May 2011.

5. In the June 24, 2003 issue of *Village Voice*, New York University's Jason King wrote an article titled "Remixing the Closet: The Down-Low Way of Knowledge," which said that men "on the down low" don't think of themselves as gay—they simply seek sex with other men, a practice they keep secret from their female partners. Similarly, Latino men who have sex with men often don't consider themselves gay as long as they play the male role and penetrate their partner.

Chapter 3

6. My brief discussion of the slander of calling gay men pedophiles may seem to imply that straight male pedophiles abuse girls and gay male pedophiles abuse boys. But this is a simplistic and inaccurate interpretation. Some straight pedophiles (many of whom are married) will sexually abuse boys because they have power issues and a need for dominance. Pedophilia is a severe psychological disorder and is separate from a person's sexual orientation.

A summary of the many professional groups' censures against Paul Cameron (who chairs and founded Family Research Institute) can be found at:

http://psychology.ucdavis.edu/rainbow/html/facts_cameron.html

An April 28, 2005 *Wall Street Journal* column by The Numbers Guy exposes the techniques Cameron uses to arrive at his flawed anti-gay figures. It can be found at:

http://online.wsj.com/article/0,,SB111461604615918400,00.
html

7. One in three women worldwide will be beaten, raped, coerced into sex or otherwise abused in her lifetime, according to L. Heise, M. Ellsberg, and M. Gottemoeller in their article "Ending Violence against Women," *Population Reports*, 1999, Series L, No. 11, Johns Hopkins University School of Public Health. A 2003 report by the United Nations Development Fund for Women made the same finding. Both noted that the rape and abuse statistics are much higher in areas where women had minimal or no rights, like sub-Saharan Africa, than in areas where women have rights. Hence the worldwide average of one in three.

8. Unfortunately, *Time* magazine did not include Jennifer Chrisler's rebuttal to Dobson's misrepresentations in its print issue, only on its website:
www.time.com/time/nation/article/0,8599,1569797,00.html
Many other websites have covered Dobson's misrepresentations in the *Time* article as well as other venues, including these:
http://mediamatters.org/research/2006/12/14/experts-say-dobsons-time-column-distorted-their/140676

An excellent interview with Judith Stacey, Ph.D., at:

www.youtube.com/watch?v=gaCCe9XVSRo

Carol Gilligan, Ph.D.'s protest against Dobson's distortions of her research:

www.youtube.com/watch?v=9NHdSVknB5Q&NR=1

Dr. Kyle Pruett's protest against Dobson's misrepresentation of his research:

www.democraticunderground.com/discuss/duboard.php?az =view_all&address=221x48164

9. Dorothy A. Greenfield, "Reproduction in same-sex couples: quality of parenting and child development," *Current Opinion in Obstetrics and Gynecology*, June 2005, Vol. 17, Issue 3. Greenfield is a clinical professor of obstetric and gynecology at Yale University School of Medicine.

10. The 2008 American Psychological Association study on gay parenting and other similar studies can be found by entering "gay parenting" as the search term at http://search.apa.org/search

Chapter 5

11. Today, many men still have religious, psychological, and/or social reasons for trying to stop or limit their masturbation and nocturnal emissions. But from a medical standpoint, unless they are having sex with their partner at least three times a week, limiting ejaculation is not a good idea. Several large-scale studies have shown that the more frequently men ejaculate, the less likely they are to get prostate cancer. See, for example, "Ejaculation Frequency and Subsequent Risk of Prostate Cancer" by Leitzmann, MD; Platz, ScD; Stampfer, MD; Willett, MD; and Giovannucci, MD, in *Journal of the American Medical Association*, 2004.

Chapter 6

12. *Biological Exuberance: Animal Homosexuality and Natural Diversity* by Bruce Bagemihl, Ph.D., deals extensively with the fascinating subject of animal homosexuality, bisexuality, and transgender manifestations.

Chapter 7

13. I conducted an extensive phone interview with Michael Bussee in 1994 for a magazine profile on him preceding the release of a PBS Point of View documentary titled *One Nation Under God.*

D. LGBT-Supportive Christian, Unitarian, and Jewish Denominations in the United States*

Ordination

The following Christian denominations allow non-celibate gay people who are in committed same-sex relationships to be ordained: Disciples of Christ, Episcopalians, Evangelical Lutherans, Metropolitan Community Church, some Quakers, United Church of Christ, United Presbyterians, Unitarians, Universalists, and Unity. Conservative Jews, Reconstructionist Jews, and Reform Jews also allow gay people to be ordained.*

Same-Sex Marriages

These Christian denominations allow their clergy to perform same-sex marriages: Disciples of Christ, Episcopalian, Evangelical Lutherans, Metropolitan Community Church, Some Quakers, United Church of Christ, Unitarians, Universalists, and Unity. Some Conservative Jews, Reconstructionist Jews, and some Reform Jews also allow their rabbis to perform same-sex marriages.*

*Accurate as of September 2012. Also, almost every denomination has LGBT support groups, and most of the non-supportive denominations have many churches and leaders working to change their policies. See Appendix A for more information.

E. COUNTRIES AND AMERICAN STATES WHERE SAME-SEX MARRIAGE IS LEGAL

(as of September 2012)

COUNTRIES

1. Netherlands, 2001

2. Belgium, 2003

3. Spain, 2005

4. Canada, 2005

5. South Africa, 2006

6. Norway, 2009

7. Sweden, 2009

8. Portugal, 2010

9. Iceland, 2010

10. Argentina, 2010

11. Denmark, 2012

Many other nations offer legal civil unions with the
same benefits as marriage.

AMERICAN STATES WHERE SAME-SEX MARRIAGE IS LEGAL

1. Massachusetts, 2004

(California briefly, until 2008)

2. Connecticut, 2008

3. Iowa, 2009

4. Vermont, 2009

(Maine briefly, until 2009)

5. New Hampshire, 2010

Washington, D.C., 2010

6. New York, 2011

ACKNOWLEDGMENTS

Many heartfelt thanks to Peggy Campolo, Monica A. Coleman, Eric Pearce, Linda Peterson, Suzi Sherman, and Virginia Boyle Valle (and her skeptical dorm mates at Trinity Western University) for reading early versions of this manuscript and making extremely helpful suggestions.

I am also grateful to Jane Halsey and Webster Williams for their first-rate proofing and editing, and to those who were kind enough to read advance copies and give their endorsement.

Thank you to Dan, for his love, encouragement, and always excellent wit.

And finally, thanks to all of you who read this book and venture to offer it to your friends who may not want to read it, but really should. I pray it will make a difference.

NOTES

CPSIA information can be obtained at www.ICGtesting.com
Printed in the USA
BVOW081441251012

303924BV00001B/2/P